THE WATCH
A COLLECTION OF POETRY

BY NORITA DITTBERNER-JAX

WHISTLING SHADE
PRESS

PO Box 7084   St. Paul   MN   55107
www.whistlingshade.com

First Edition, Second Printing
July 2011

Cover Design, Lauren Bartel

The following poems appeared in the publications listed here,
some in slightly different versions:

"Einstein in San Francisco" won first prize in the Talking Stick
Competition, 2006, and was published in the anthology.

Artword Quarterly: "Repairing the Body"

The Dos Passos Review: "Meditation on the Body"

Dust and Fire: "Bathing the Child" and "Saying Good-bye"

Minnesota Poetry Calendar: "Thanksgiving"

Saint Paul Almanac: "Landscape"

Sidewalks: "Ultrasound," "Leaving for the Lake," and "Gargoyle"

Water-Stone: "Regret for Things Lost", "Sundays," and "Landscape"

Whistling Shade: "How to Live"

I am deeply grateful to those who have sustained me in the long work of writing poetry, especially Eugene Jax, husband and first reader, my children and stepchildren, my sisters and brothers, writers, and dear friends, especially Diane Olson, wife of Harlan.

Thanks to the Minneapolis Institute of Arts, the William Hood Dunwoody Fund, for permission to use Cezanne's The Chestnut Trees at Jas de Bouffan *on the cover and to Laura Beadoin for her careful copy editing of the manuscript. Without the talent and energy of my dear friend and fellow poet, Sharon Chmielarz, this book would be a poorer thing.*

And, finally, to editor Lauren Bartel and publisher Joel Van Valin, gratitude for your commitment and courage in embarking on the adventurous seas of small press publishing — good news for us all.

*For my people
the living and the dead.*

Contents

I. Voices in the Stairwell

II. The Solace of the Dark

III. Night Sky from the Window

IV. The Old Joy

I.
Voices in the Stairwell

All the Lost Homes

That first house, the colonnades, the beamed ceiling
is the lost life of childhood, the house I can't enter,
except to record its tender and seamy details.

The first house of my marriage, pink rambler,
a replica of our neighbor's, another loss,
life of the bride, first Christmas, new mother.

The family home on Lombard, the rambling Victorian
that held us like a recurring dream, mysterious light
and leafy darkness, then stopped holding us: the divorce.

I stayed on, a displaced person in the lost life of Lombard,
then slowly gained back one corner at a time, alone and not-alone,
the children and I, the back and forth of shared custody.

A man came with his dog, Muffin; we walked the city,
talking about the houses of our lives until all our rooms were
    known,
and the house on Lombard slipped into the river of lost lives.

Now in the duplex on Goodrich, we live the close life.
The large sunny living room opens into the interior
where we cook and eat, wash and sleep, a found life.

I think there is a life ahead, the last lost life, the one in which we're
happy and the kids come and go, where Muffin dies at Christmas
    time
and we cry ourselves to sleep and Muffin joins what is lost to us.

But this morning, I can see that the plaster won't hold, brick
will crumble, and another generation will say, "Did they really
live here?" and this beloved house, another relic of the lost life.

Thanksgiving

They come, slamming the doors of their little cars
and bearing covered dishes, our offspring,

their spouses and roommates, all gathered
at the Thanksgiving board,

the table a pleasure, a beauty, a groan, the turkey laid out
in front of us, the handmade stuffing,

potatoes riced and creamed, the cranberries
that slid out of the can classic as Greek pillars,

ten of us, laughing, elbow to elbow, what more could I ask?
This loneliness is a way of preparing

for the next generation and remembrance of the dead.
I miss them both today.

I serve the pies, apple and pumpkin, wanting to send a piece
or two on to the other side.

Our ranks are thin, they want plumping up. This is the time
between the old and the new,

a thin layer between grief and possibility. Out of this longing
came all the generations.

Walking Pike Island

We move separately through sheets of snow
gathering in the field that lies between two rivers,
the Mississippi and the Minnesota.

Begun in mildness, the snow slows us
and you ask, should we turn back, but I want to go on,
want to reach the point of confluence.

We follow the shoreline, the river quicksilver against snow
and bark. We veer slightly, arrive suddenly at the point.
Pike called this a natural site for a fortress,

but the Dakota called it "center of the earth."
I think it is a marrying ground, joining water
and land, river and river, where things come together.

If we were getting married again, I would choose this spot.
Your people would walk the Mississippi side
and my people the Minnesota side

and we would make confluence at this site.
But we are already married, so we stomp our feet and bow
to the waters flowing together.

January, Two Weeks In

We cannot part with it.
In early January, we slide our perfect tree outside,
bare of lights and ornaments, all the cardinals and finches,
the parrot from Brazil, the apples red with promise, packed away.

We stand the tree smack in the middle of the front yard
where it rests in low winter light, snow softening its branches,
but in the spike of needle, from spine to spire, the memory
of wilderness.

I wish we had a whole stand of pine in our yard,
gathered like friends in time of need. But we have only this,
a fir tree, our tannenbaum, to keep the memory of forest,
of bear and deer, the earth's time,
long and steady.

Ultrasound

Shadow baby, intent
upon your thumb, rolling
in gestational waters,
how your mother smiles
seeing your profile, your nose.
The technician measures
the size of your brain,
the chambers of your heart.
I hold my breath,
but, seeing you in all your perfection,
your mother just laughs.

Saying Good-Bye to my Daughter

I wish they were neater, our good-byes.
The babies, the dog, our husbands,
all up against the door.

The best thing would be the quick
kiss, click of the seatbelt,
a final wave.

Instead we fall into each other's arms
and all the good-byes of the past
echo in the valley between us:

Baby girl, born at midnight, spirited
down the dark corridor, the first
time I missed you.

The mother and the joint custody kid
so practiced at packing;
the child who didn't want to go to school
on Monday morning.

At the front door now, with all
that clamoring to move on, we stop
to enact it all again.

Then you return to a city near water
and I re-order the house with all its light
and the shadows like draperies
I pull against the dark.

Regret for Things Lost

Not husbands or home,
not umbrellas, not the keys I've left
scattered widely as male seed
in the world,

but a shirt stolen from the clothesline
years ago, a shirt in which I felt
perfectly myself, the ache
of that blue-striped theft.

And bracelets. One from my brother
of antique silver that I wore
on my wedding day; the other
from my husband, a simple
gold band, ring for my wrist, both lost,
one in Bemidji, one in Cornwall.

Blue clip earrings, the only ones I ever loved,
sacrificed for a more severe version
of myself, the woman I was, lost,
with all her accoutrements.

There are so many things
in this culture, so many disposables,
surely there are replacements.

I wish it were enough that I remember
the blue stones
of my youth, enough
that what I put on is a flag
I'm waving to the world,
enough to be
a woman who has been given bracelets
of silver and gold,
but something in me is willful,
wanting them back,

hungry to hold them again,
my things,
jewelry in my palm,
shirt on the clothesline where I left it.

Amsterdam

For Eugene

1.

You, asleep in your trousers, one leg bent
and crossed at the knee, feet pale
as fish out of water. Your breath comes
in soft growls, but this time I won't jar you
to change your position. Go on
in your rest in the white room
of an Amsterdam afternoon.

Outside the window, bicyclists pedal,
their chains droning like bees;
the waters of the canal lie still.
Downtown the prostitutes who posed
in their windows last night
yawn and stretch in their shifts,
the push-up bra and thong abandoned
in the corner.

A pause. Siesta for a northern city.
Voices in the stairwell die out.
A hundred years ago, this hotel
was an orphanage, and something of it
remains in the long hallway
of doors, each with a half-moon step,
a little home.

2.

The row houses of Amsterdam
rise tall and narrow,
each one distinct in gable
and baluster, like the friezes
of my grade school years
when we each drew a scene
from the long life of Jesus,
the length of the blackboard,
and it turned out altogether
beautiful, the way Amsterdam
turned out, each narrow house
separate and together,
and at the roof line, the highest
pitch of each unit, a hook,
a hitch for a piano or sofa,
to be hoisted up on thick
nautical ropes. Walking the city,
we saw wallboard angled
like a UFO over the pavement
and rowboats parked on streets
of water, the whole circuitous
route of canals running
like nerves through the city.

3.

Anne Frank's house, the secret annex
on the canal at 265 Prinsengracht,
the family hiding in the walls like bats,
never seeing daylight and the girl documenting
her life vividly, her comments on
her father's business of spices and jams,
"As long as you're in the food business,
why not make candy?" and the opening
to her last notebook, called Worldly Advice,
"To be a person, you must have flair!"

Seeing the annex fifty years later, how
life went on allowing the girl to record
her time as if it were normal, the writing so
lively, it softens the fact of her death.

She had a mind that ranged
even while imprisoned. But that terrible descent
at Bergen-Belsen, no way to hold on:
"I have lost everyone," she told her friend
through the fence.

What happened here has been made into
a museum. There's nothing to see
but empty rooms.

On the street,
I look at the gray waters of the canal,
not the same water Anne knew.
This water has run with the waters
of the whole world.

4.

We sit in a room, very dark,
and watch a film of the sun
setting at twilight; no sound
in a dark room. Then a woman's
voice as clear as a flute begins,
"I'll be seeing you,
in all the old familiar places..."
The sun dissolves into pinks
and lavender, a channel opens
and flows freely, a sense of time
running out and nothing to do
but wipe my face
with an old Kleenex
and enter the hot afternoon
of the future.

5.

Our last night, we spend in the park in our neighborhood
and watch a big-screen Aida on the side of a truck,
grand opera on a semi, all of us together.
The Dutch eat cheese with wine and smoke cigarettes
into the blue night air. There is a letting down
for us, as if we have stayed long enough to be at home
among them, the way a place attaches itself
once you sit still. We walk home; the Dutch
pedal their bicycles, a kaleidoscope of spokes,
wheels, spinning into the summer night.

Sundays

My mother entered our house with all her good days gone,
nothing left but to live out the bad,
her whole life a streak of good luck next to this.

We pulled the wheelchair up the front steps,
and the children came to greet her,
frightened by her stillness, no relation

to the grandmother who did tip-overs with them
on the carpet. I brought in the commode, pushed it
to the corner until she needed it,

then lifted her out and sat her down.
When she finished, I gathered her up in my arms,
arranging and rearranging her garments

and returned her to the wheelchair
where she composed herself
back into the stroke.

The look we exchanged before the moment
of holding, our eyes level and straight.
Holding her longer than I needed to

(she always was good to be near),
the long moment of holding my mother,
her broken house of bones.

Shoring Up

To be with you
walking the wide
boulevards
blindingly white
in stone and shine;
to pass a cafe
where a waiter unfurls
a white tablecloth
like a flag saluting
the bread and wine
to come; to cross
and recross the low bridges
of the Seine and behold!
its sheen turns
midnight blue,
the shade of the Evening
in Paris perfume
I bought my mother
at Woolworth's,
ahh, let it come,
let it all come.

II.
The Solace of the Dark

Meditation on the Body

How it presents itself to the world
combed or careless, the layers
of cloth covering the smooth skin.

The body in lovemaking,
the rosy interior revealed, the desire
to be known thoroughly,
nipple and foreskin.

The body in its frailty,
arriving for surgery at an unsuitable
hour, a parking ramp orange-lit
to prevent murder, and in a cubicle
the size of your closet, removing
everything until you are down
to synapse, pulse, breath.

The body as cathedral--sanctuary,
dome, cloister —
coming full circle
from my early schooling,
the body as temple, the holy.

This body of ours,
this gorgeous flowering whose roots
pump life to every cell,
the way in
and out, a door.

Crossing

For Don Belleau

Now I see how the living begin
the passage: Information
arrives, the measured cadence
of bad news, an announcement
as sudden as the warning
on the loudspeaker, "The store
will be closing in five minutes."

If you sleep, you remember
with your first breath upon waking;
you weigh yourself, but what use
is the scale, artifact of an earlier life?

You live out your days amid the clocks
and calendars of earth, but your mind
is on the old verities,
death, truth.

Those who love you bear this,
watch as you lay aside one object after
another, wristwatch, gloves,
the contents of your life taking on dignity
as you sweeten into your passing.

The Vigil

In Memoriam,
Harlan Olson

1.

You come up our walk,
our best friend,
hapless with cancer.
Snow flurries drop
from an overcast sky.
We need a patch of green,
a little resurrection.

How easily we laugh in the car,
the four of us; like children
in church, covering our mouths
against the outburst of mischief,
everything hilarious.

You sit in our front yard
on the plastic Adirondack chairs
smoking a cigar. The smoke engulfs
you and then is borne away.
The limbs of the great oak
shake their fists at heaven
or reach for it.

Remember when I ran into the two of you
drinking beer in O'Gara's?
You had urged him to call me and there
we were, arranging a date,
hearts thumping in surprise.
The first New Year's Eve,
I made crab mousse and we fished
the Drambuie out from behind the stove,

the first hours of that good year.

Each time you hug me,
you hold me a moment.
I feel your bones, the timbers
of your house.

Your life, all the rituals
of family and home, walls
to be painted, so many bolts to be
tightened and loosened. Whatever
is taken away, the strength to clean
your own gutters, your favorite meals
replaced by Ensure,
is enough.

Midsummer. The coleus in their pots
grown so soon to fullness.
We sit in the summerhouse,
the four of us. You say little
but your eyes follow the low bounce
of our voices. The long pull
of twilight.

2.

Waking to see the maple
emerge from darkness.

Loving each other, our bodies easy as fish
if we're lucky, and if we're not, still
lucky.

A walk in the neighborhood, the quiet
porches, a string of Christmas lights in May.

These days we live close, as if to venture far
would strain our resources.

Sunday night we sit alone in a cathedral. "Keep me
as the apple of your eye. Hide me

in the shadow of your wings." The psalms,
The solace of the dark.

3.

When your friend is dying,
all the stoplights are red
for you. The driver in the car
turning right, the chatting couple
in the next lane, have all the time
in the world while you grip
the steering wheel white-knuckled.
You are a courteous person,
yet you give them the finger
under the dashboard. All they see
is a woman behind the wheel,
jaw line locked as a fist,
even as you realize that no
hurry of yours will change
his life, emptying faster
than you can drive.

4.

He died facing the light.

You and his sons smoked the last
of his cigars in the screen house.

I sat at the dining room table
with the women.

The neighbor, the one who buzzed
the edges of his lawn all summer,

went house to house, asking
for quiet.

5.

Two whole salmon with grapes for eyes,
a wheel of cheese, gallons of pasta
with tomatoes and feta — one glorious spread.

"Ninety-eight bucks for a fish!" says the man
behind me in the checkout line.
I look up and see others eyeing our order

with frank interest. The woman behind him
asks, "Having a party?" I hear myself say,
"Our best friend died."

The truth is leaking out everywhere.

He didn't get to stand in enough lines,
making good-natured talk
at the checkout counter.

His wife will be alone, as these lovers
of food are, widowed, divorced, making small
pools of community wherever they go.

6.

Late August. The sun paralyzed
at high noon, the days flat
as a movie set.

Then we enter the flow of traffic
on the freeway, turn up at the desks
our lives require of us.

The furnace kicks in for the first time.
The great oak is shaking
its leaves loose,

ready to bear
the coming winter, a harshness
it will suffer and survive.

7.

I'm learning death,
funeral by funeral
the way students practice
a new word, over and over.

Each friend, each relative
breaks down
the mind's resistance:
This is no fluke.

The long box,
the urns of ash and fragments,
the poster board
of photos,

the whole fiefdom of a life
reduced to this: Ah,
maybe so, maybe so
even to me.

Landscape

I drive across the High Bridge with St. Paul sprawling
before me, built on hills like Rome itself.

I see the cathedral piercing the sky and think
of its domed interior, its mysterious recesses

and imagine it imploding, collapsing into the nave,
and how the hills of St. Paul would go on being hills,

how everything would compose itself briefly
around the absence of the cathedral

and then just go on. This is the first time
I have accepted the idea of my own death.

III.
Night Sky from the Window

Ancient Rooms

1.

I wandered into a Roman bath
and thought of the men who bathed
within its steep walls, arranging for trade
and prosperity; thought of the women
who rinsed them off from great pitchers
of water, gone, all of them gone.

I looked up at the single window and saw
the wheels of traffic on Rue Saint-Jacques
and people passing on the pavement,
their mouths moving without sound.

The sun sent shafts of light pooling into
the middle of the chamber, offering itself,
an invitation. I stepped into it,
one woman in the census of the world.

2.

A room used now for string quartets
at noon, bone-white Roman walls
around which pale medieval statues
stare, not one of them whole.

To the west, the heads of the kings
of Judah mounted on pedestals,
a chorus of judgment, mute
and terrible.

To the east and south, the saints,
some without torsos,
some without arms, even the stone
hem of a robe cut off.

What concerto could offset the white
carnage, everything human bleached out?
Afterward on the street,
I want to deny myself nothing,
live voraciously
against the time to come.

Redeemer

The time is after the beginning and before
the middle. Pilate has already handed him over,
but here is what the evangelists did not record,
a pause in the story.

Jesus sits in an alcove of darkness, legs crossed,
one hand supporting his face, the other
resigned on his lap.

In front of him, the clarity
of the cross he will take up soon. On the floor,
the scourge, the hammer, the nails.

Jesus in his predicament, no
exit, the air of resignation, as if the next thing
will be a sigh, nothing to tear the curtain
of the temple or unsettle the graves of the dead,

but one deep breath: Who wanted to be a redeemer
anyway? Then, uncrossing his legs
and, both hands on his thighs, rising.

Man of Sorrows, 1560
Luis de Morales

How to Live

A hundred years ago, the fire
of a Ukrainian foundry
forged this cross.

You brought it from Kiev,
the crucifix passed
from one generation
to another, the corpus
worn and shining,
a landscape of valleys
and hills and the long
geography of limbs.

It fits my hand perfectly;
my thumb worries the head,
a comfort, as it was for others
who held it in sickness
or hid it during persecution.

Sometimes now I am tired,
worn down with caring. I want
hours alone, the radio mute.

Then I wonder, which way?
Preserve myself?
Or like the little cross from Kiev,
let the blessing of hands
leave its shine upon me.

Lucretia

She still holds the knife
in one hand, and steadies herself
with a cord in the other.

We do not see her husband,
but he is there, powerless to protect her
from the rapist, or her own despair.

The brocade robe falls open,
framing the white chemise,
the private interior.

The wash of blood
from the wound she inflicts on herself
mirrors the other wound.

Rembrandt painted her at the end
of his life, acquainted, as he was,
with terrible loss.

How he troubled over her eyes,
more sorrowful
than any crucifixion.

Lucretia, 1666
Rembrandt van Rijn

Monet, Van Gogh, at Home

The wonder that Monet
had time to paint, the vast
size of the garden and across
the road, the Japanese pond,
a man enchanted with nature —
flowers, water, haystacks, and
light! A blind man's obsession
with light, every slant of the sundial
documented, time filtering
light.

What a life! Two wives
the second with six children!
No wonder the huge table
in the dining room, fourteen chairs,
all canary yellow; the blue-
and white-tiled kitchen, large
and commodious, festooned
with copper pots;
the large bedroom overlooking
the garden: to throw open
these shutters in the morning!
So much life!

Modest, difficult, van Gogh
thought himself one link in the chain
and took the yellow house at Arles,
on Place Lamartine, hoping
others would come. A table
and two chairs and just enough
left for broth and coffee.

Gauguin fled after two months
when Vincent chased him
with a razor. He painted
"Gauguin's Chair" empty except
for a lit candle, in memory
of the failure.

Toward the end, he painted
the vestibule near his room,
the yard where he was confined,
night sky from his window.

The Charleston Room

I was a girl when I stood behind the rope,
staring at the drawing room, my only
companion the hum
of a humidifier.

The windows were heavily draped
in yellow satin, but gave no light
and no one entered this room,

but if they had, arrangements
of furniture would hold them:
sit here for tea, here, play
whist by candlelight, or collapse
on the fainting couch.

Later when I read Jane Austin,
I knew just where the heroine
would sit with her sisters
that world born in my head years before,

so different from mine, where lilacs
picked in the morning faded by evening,
and the maidens ran headlong
into their lives.

The Bath

The water in the basin holds
their attention. The girl's arm
is braced cautiously against
her mother's knee, toes tipping
the surface of the water.

The mother's hands
are large and persuasive, caressing
the foot into water.

Their heads touch, no distance
to cross, one is holding the other,
one is being held.

Against such vulnerability,
the bold stripe of the mother's dress,
the wallpaper's roses,
a single blossom in a square
of carpet.

How everything conspires to defend
that innocence, the skin so pale,
the white towel draped
to protect the child even from eyes
that have been invited in.

The Child's Bath, 1893
Mary Cassatt

After Frida's Family Tree

Everything gets into the painting.
Cameos of grandparents float
like heavy balloons in the sky,
the set from Mexico soars above
the tiny mountain range,
while the Germans hover above
the ocean they crossed.
Frida's mother and father pose
in their wedding clothes, the bride
in white with a cutaway of the baby
in her womb for our x-ray eyes.
And the girl, naked and sturdy,
standing four-square in the courtyard
with a lemon tree grazing her knee?
That's Frida, too, claiming
her inheritance. But already
her eyebrows are moving toward
each other like two trains
before the collision.

My Grandparents, My Parents and I, 1936
Frida Kahlo

Sculpture of a Woman

She is sitting without name or clothes
on the museum floor.

If the artist had left the bronze
in its natural state,
not painted her fleshtone.

If she were standing,
on a pedestal, instead of sitting
with her slender legs tucked under
like wings at rest. But this:

Her stunning nakedness,
the hip and breast line whiter
than the shoulders or legs, so we imagine
the clothing she wore in the sun.

The veins of her arms, the thickened pads
of her feet, the path the comb took
through waves of hair.

Her gaze turned inward, as if this display
were a humiliation she expected.
The small breasts, the slight
slack at the waist —

I want to get the blanket
from the trunk of the car,
cover her, give her a name.

Eve.

Untitled Bronze #1
John De Andrea

IV.
The Old Joy

Stoplight

The sudden fragrance of lilac,
the smell of cut grass through
the open window.

My shoulders rest easy,
joints smooth as dancers
in their sockets.

I think of kissing,
the call and response
of flesh and bone.

Then I remember them
missing their first spring,
not in earth
but in air.

The sky above the tree line
dissolves into lavender
at the horizon
where they live now.

I can't take you with me.
The light turns amber.

Gargoyle

For Eric

I.

Sometimes, before class, I feel shy
about being in front of them.
If I had a way out, I'd take it,
just as they would. Then I plunge
into class — they turn in late papers
and no matter what structure
I've set up, baskets, bins,
they hand them to me,
wanting an exchange of the eyes.

Sometimes in class, a student's face
changes, a slight shift of tectonic plates
exposes an angle of grief almost
unbearable.

I think, what if they all unmask,
what will I do then?

II.

I wanted light to pour in
from the windows of my classroom,
but the television is mounted there,
its cords tangled like intestine.

I wanted curves, the desks in half-
moons, but the long train
of fluorescent light burns a hole
in the dark.

What I wanted was so grand,
I forgot the postcard of the gargoyle
I taped to the podium to absorb
any misery coming my way,
saying, send them on up!
Your detentions, the trouble
at home, every bridge in your life
that comes up short,

feed them to the monster, let him
chew on it while you do
the mind's work of reading
and moving your hand across paper.

III.

Their heads are bent to paper, copying out
William Blake's "The Lamb" and "The Tyger"

on opposite sides of the notebooks, adjoining
poems. They will graduate in three weeks and most

I will not see again, but here, now,
we have the odd affection, the familiarity

and shyness of teacher and student, this closeness
over poems by mad William who lives on and on

becoming the gift I give these students,
and the gift they give themselves.

Be accurate, I say
and make them as beautiful as you can

and they do; the room is very quiet.
In the courtyard the lilacs open.

In Sickness

The monkey of pain climbs the cage
of my husband's body. I push fluids,
make sweet puddings to entice him to eat.

When he sleeps, I practice
sitting at my desk. The open
closet door holds my empty clothes.

My shoes in their compartments
march in pairs down the door
heading toward me.

I could get up and shut the door
but I don't. I practice
a new reserve,

reticence against
tomorrow, what
it may hold.

Repairing the Body

1.
I can stay in these four walls
with the bad news, but I can't
go into the world
without you.

2.
You take nothing with you,
your keys, your wallet, your glasses,
not even your wedding ring.
A door swings open.

3.
In the waiting room, a stranger
talks to me, but the sound is shut off.
Hands cut into the clock's face;
the sun rises.

4.
Our children, your sister, our friend
join me; you have almost as many people
as the Mexican family. The waves of English
and Spanish comfort me.

5.
I cannot stop thanking the doctor
who fixed you. The crease
in his trousers is precise, his nails,
immaculate. Praise him.

6.

Five days later, as I prepare
to take you home, the news
of Paulo's death. How ignorant
we were last month talking
with him, death hidden
like a microphone behind
the curtains, picking up
each lively word.

7.

Silence entered me this year;
I didn't rush to cover it, but let it fall.
Gradually it settled like sunlight
on our sofa.

8.

Two months since we thought
you might die, since I remembered
to dream. But now the night
holds no terror. You mend, your stitches
the railroad tracks crossing
a country I love.

9.

Lying there afterwards
I feel the perfect sense
our bodies make, and it is good,
all good.

10.

The smell of coffee, the stretch
of my body in the morning,
the old joy.

Leaving for the Lake

We're doing the disappearing act, folding
our urban life back into the walls
of this house like a Murphy bed.

I clean up the kitchen, wipe the sauce
from the stove, pack up
the bread, no crumbs for ten days.

I move quickly from one surface to the other,
fascinated by this removal of our effects,
my hands, sly thieves making a clean sweep.

When we finally pile into the car, I turn back
wanting to see who we were before
we moved onto water.

In that second, I remember Lot's wife
who had enough brain left from the fury of packing
to look back and see Sodom and Gomorrah burning.

She was punished for her curiosity.
I am luckier: behind me the house bakes
in July heat and hardens to salt.

The Boat

We slip through the darkness, feeling in the boat's rocking
the heaviness of water, under us, around us;

a halo of light in the west, the barest of moons,
the least moon possible.

Docks already gone to darkness, houses barely visible,
but the lives lived there stand in clear panes of light.

We are four friends, two marriages, taking a turn
on the lake. The wind blows up a fierce smell of water and fish.

We are quiet, surrounded by water, rocking
in the darkness of the boat, frail as moths.

Desk

Just now,
the study where the quiet is
and my raw poems,
their edges curling
in July heat, the desk clear
as my brow when I enter
its radiant field.

Then, as if
from stage left, the light dims;
my mind returns
to the classroom
and joins my body so
quietly,

no one hears it
slide into place,
that neat
click.

Afternoon

Quietly,
not disturbing
the silence of the sofa,
the chairs,
the hands of the clock
on the mantel poised one minute
before the hour,

I come into the room flooded
with light.
Beyond the window,
the school yard empty
of children, as our house
is now.

We live here alone.
You are reading
from your pile of books
when I cross over
stepping into angles
of light.

Einstein in San Francisco

Post-mastectomy, you exercise to music
in the living room, while I read the Sunday paper
on the sofa, the Pacific long as the horizon
behind me. Yo Yo Ma is playing
an Appalachian lament. In my mind
I see his head bowed, his arm slowly drawing
the sweetness out of the cello.

A wild, dark energy
is pushing the universe apart.
Eventually, it will implode, a slide
into senescence.

I heard the diagnosis in a hotel room
in a strange city; the flashing of the telephone's
red light, a wild dark energy.
I came to be in the same state,
the same room with you, in the city
you've made your home,
galaxies from the high school in Frogtown
where we met.

Einstein called his theory a blunder,
but all the signs point to his genius:
the universe will cool and darken.
In 30 billion years, it will collapse
in on itself.

You're on your feet now, up against
the dining room wall, raising your arm
ten times. Wincing, brave girl.

It's no news to us that the universe
is expanding. We'll never live
in the same city again. We airlift
in and out of each other's lives
and in the long interval between flights,

we telephone our pleasure
and sorrow. There's time enough
for us to turn sixty, even seventy,
maybe eighty. Remember. Call me.

Daughter on the Mountain

Taking T'ai Chi Chih,
I'm learning
balance, shifting
my weight from one foot
to the other,
making platters, balls
with my hands,
daughter on the mountain,
daughter in the valley.

The master tells me to keep
my mind on my feet and shift
my weight so
completely
that I could lift
one foot off
the ground.

My feet obey, but my mind
wanders back
to Jerusalem to the top
of the Old City,
the story of Mohammed,
how he rested his foot on a rock
before climbing the ladder of light,
pushing off
into the vault of the sky,
his night journey to heaven.

Rocking my body, forward
and back, I'm poised
for flight, like Mohammed.
The joy of it! How difficult
to keep my mind on my feet,
to stay in this world,
with my head full
of Mohammed and the terrible
temptation to rise.

Anniversary

Father: I remember your death
not from the calendar
but from the light
in late winter,
how the sun glared through the branches
of trees in the weeks
following the funeral,
no place to hide, nothing
to soften the plain fact
of your death, you,
felled by something bigger
than yourself,
and fast, seven hours from onset to death;
you, still.

In the years since, I've gone my own way.
I remember mother more often
than you, and for this
I have no remedy.
The things you gave, love of the city, passion
for music which in me turned to language,
stay with me.

I'm married now to a man with mother's gentleness
and your fierceness. You two would fight,
I know.
When we traveled to Germany, our ancestral home,
I manufactured dreams as if I were a theatre,
reel after reel, nightmares, fantasies,
all the parts of my life
flowing into each other,
but one gem,
one sweet dream in which you and mother appear
as yourselves, vigorous, hearty,
my richest inheritance.

Birthday

I drive across town, past the freeway, stoplights, each one
a milestone from childhood to my old neighborhood in Frogtown.
Spring has just stopped holding its breath and the soft wind barely
ruffles the flag on the school. I forgot how flat the streets are,
even the hill where I daringly lifted my hands from the handlebars
of my bike is no hill at all. The houses are small and bony, even
our house of four bedrooms seems to have shrunk. I drive past
the church to the avenue the hearse took with the bodies of my
mother and father, and enter their town with its low houses and
tiny skyscrapers, the untrampled grass. The car seems to steer
itself along the narrow path to their street. I clean off their common
stone and place the single yellow tulip between their names,
Doris, Otto, then the long music of Dittberner. I stay long
enough to say thank you, for my life, the sixth of seven children,
born in my mother's 47th year, a world of ordinary houses and
minimal geography, a lively mother, a singing father and a
generous offering of brothers and sisters. I drive home, back
across the intersections and the freeway to my neighborhood
of weighty houses and hills to live out the rest of my life.